First World War
and Army of Occupation
War Diary
France, Belgium and Germany

16 DIVISION
Divisional Troops
81 Sanitary Section
18 December 1915 - 31 March 1917

WO95/1968/2

The Naval & Military Press Ltd
www.nmarchive.com
Published in association with The National Archives

Published by

The Naval & Military Press Ltd

Unit 10 Ridgewood Industrial Park,

Uckfield, East Sussex,

TN22 5QE England

Tel: +44 (0) 1825 749494

www.naval-military-press.com

www.nmarchive.com

This diary has been reprinted in facsimile from the original. Any imperfections are inevitably reproduced and the quality may fall short of modern type and cartographic standards.

© **Crown Copyright**
Images reproduced by permission of The National Archives, London, England, 2015.

Contents

Document type	Place/Title	Date From	Date To
Heading	WO95/1968/2 16 Divn Div Troops 81 Sanitary Sec. 1915 Dec-1917 Mar		
Heading	16th Division 81st Sanitary Section Dec 1915-1917 Mar To 2 Army		
Heading	16th Division F/255/1 Summarised But Not Copied San Sect 81 Vol I 121/7911 S December 1915-Dec.1916		
Heading	War Diary Or Intelligence Summary Of O.C. 81st Sanitary Section 16th. Division From Dec 18th 1915 to Dec 31st 1915 Volume-1		
War Diary		18/12/1915	31/12/1915
Heading	16th Division 16 Div F/255/2. San. Sect, 81 Vol 2 Jan 1916		
Heading	81 Sanitary Section Jan Vol		
War Diary		01/01/1916	28/01/1916
War Diary		01/01/1916	31/01/1916
Heading	16th Div 81st. Sany Section Feb 1916		
Heading	San. Sect. 81 Vol. 3		
Heading	War Diary Or Intelligence Summary. Of The 81st. Sanitary Section (16th Division) February Volume 3		
War Diary		01/02/1916	29/02/1916
War Diary		27/02/1916	28/02/1916
Heading	War Diaries Of 81st Sanitary Section-16th Division For The Months Of March And April 1916		
Heading	War Diary. Of The 81st Sanitary Section 16th Division Volume 4 Sheets 1+2.		
War Diary		01/03/1916	08/03/1916
War Diary		02/03/1916	26/03/1916
War Diary		14/03/1916	29/03/1916
War Diary		27/03/1916	31/03/1916
Heading	War Diary Or Intelligence Summary Of The 16th. Divisional Sanitary Section. For April 1916. Volume 4.		
War Diary		01/04/1916	30/04/1916
Heading	War Diary Or Intelligence Summary Of The 81st Sanitary Section (16th Division) Vol. 6 Sheets 1 & 2		
War Diary		01/05/1916	31/05/1916
Heading	War Diary of 81st. Sanitary Section RAMC TF (16th. division) June 1916. Vol 7. (Sheet 1 & 2)		
War Diary		01/06/1916	30/06/1916
Heading	16th Division 81st Sany Section 1st. July To 31st. July 1916. Volume.		
War Diary		01/07/1916	31/07/1916
Heading	War Diary. 81st. Sanitary Section Month Of August, 1916. Volume 9		
War Diary		01/08/1916	31/08/1916
Heading	War Diary 81st Sanitary Section RAMC For Month Of September, 1916. Volume 10.		
War Diary		01/09/1916	30/09/1916
Heading	War Diary Month Of October, 1916. Volume 11 81st Sanitary Section		
War Diary		01/10/1916	31/10/1916

Miscellaneous	Drinking Water Supplies In The 16th. Divisional Area.	01/10/1916	01/10/1916
Miscellaneous	Sanitation.	14/10/1916	14/10/1916
Diagram etc	Sanitary Section 16th Division		
Diagram etc	Type "C" Incinerator		
Diagram etc	Mens Latrine Scale 1/2 = 1 Foot		
Heading	War Diary. For Month Of November, 1916. Volume 12. 81st Sanitary Section R.A.M.C.		
War Diary	Westoutre	01/11/1916	30/11/1916
Miscellaneous	A.D.M.S., 16th. Division.	22/11/1916	22/11/1916
Diagram etc	Advanced Water Supply-Kemmel.		
Heading	War Diary For Month Of December, 1916. Volume 13 R.A.M.C. 81st Sanitary Secn		
War Diary	In The Field	01/12/1916	31/12/1916
Heading	War Diary For Month Of January, 1917. Volume 14 R.A.M.C. 81st Sanitary Section		
War Diary	In The Field	01/01/1917	31/01/1917
Heading	War Diary. For Month Of February. 1917. Volume 15 81st Sanitary Section R.A.M.C.		
War Diary	In The Field	01/02/1917	28/02/1917
Heading	War Diary For Month Of March, 1917. Volume 16 81st Sanitary Sector R.A.M.C.		
War Diary	In the Field	01/03/1917	31/03/1917

16 DIVN
DIV TROOPS
81 SANITARY SEC. 1915 DEC — 1917 MAR

WO 95/1968/2

16TH DIVISION

81ST SANITARY SECTION

DEC 1915 - ~~DEC 1916~~
1917 MAR

To 2 ARMY

16th November

F/255/1

Saw. Sect: 81
Pol: I

summarised but not copied

131/7911

S
December 1915
—
Dec. 1916.

War Diary
or
Intelligence Summary
of
O.C. 81st Sanitary Section
16th Division

From Dec 18th 1915 to Dec 31st 1915

Volume :- 1.

Army Form C. 2118.

Page 1.

WAR DIARY
or
INTELLIGENCE SUMMARY.
(Erase heading not required.)

Instructions regarding War Diaries and Intelligence Summaries are contained in F.S. Regs., Part II. and the Staff Manual respectively. Title pages will be prepared in manuscript.

Hour, Date, Place		Summary of Events and Information	Remarks and references to Appendices
Dec 18th 1915	10.30 a.m.	Left DUKE OF YORK'S SCHOOL, CHELSEA, the Headquarters of the 1st London (City of London) Sanitary Company, in charge and Command of the 15th L. Division proceeding for service overseas. Section, to join the 16th Division proceeding for service overseas. Marched to SOUTH KENSINGTON Railway Station, District Railway and entrained for SOUTHAMPTON.	Proceeded according to orders received from MAJOR H.S. FREMLIN RAMCT O.C. 1st London (City of London) Sanitary Company
	11.15 a.m.	ARRIVED at WATERLOO, and entrained for SOUTHAMPTON.	
	3.15 p.m.	Arrived at SOUTHAMPTON.	
	3.30 p.m.	Reported to Embarkation Officer at SOUTHAMPTON.	orders received from Embarkation Commandants.
	4.0 p.m.	Embarked on H.M. Transport "MAIDAN".	
	8.30 p.m.	Transport left SOUTHAMPTON. During the voyage received instructions regarding disembarkation from O.C. Troops. P.A.	orders received from O.C. Troops.
Dec 19th 1915	5.0 a.m.	Arrival off HAVRE.	
	9.30 a.m.	Disembarkation commenced.	
	6.15 p.m.	Marched from quay to Point 6.	
	6.30 p.m.	Arrived at "Point 6". Drew rations for 2 days, and the 9 am Ration and entrained.	orders received from DAQMG
	9.45 p.m.	Train left HAVRE. Proceeds via ABBEVILLE, ST OMER, (At HAZEBROUCK to FOUQUEREUIL.	
Dec 20th 1915	6.30 p.m.	Arrived FOUQUEREUIL Railway Station (Map 36 13, "B" Square, 2nd Edition, E13d.)	orders received from R.T.O. nothing
	9.30 p.m.	Left FOUQUEREUIL Railway Station and marched to DROUVIN.	

(7399) W4141—463. 400,000. 9/14. H.&J. Ltd. Forms/C. 2118/10.

Army Form C. 2118.

WAR DIARY
or
INTELLIGENCE SUMMARY.
(Erase heading not required.)

Page 2.

Instructions regarding War Diaries and Intelligence Summaries are contained in F.S. Regs., Part II. and the Staff Manual respectively. Title pages will be prepared in manuscript.

Hour, Date, Place	Summary of Events and Information	Remarks and references to Appendices
Dec 20th 1915 10.45 p.m.	Arrived DROUVIN. (Map 36.B 1st Series 2nd Edition K4c). P.H. P.H.	
Dec 21st 1915 9.0 a.m.	Reported arrival to A.D.M.S.	
Dec 21st 1915 — Dec 30th 1915	Engaged on sanitary duties in connection with the various units of the 16th Division.	
Dec 31st	8.30 a.m. Dispatched advanced party from DROUVIN to AUCHY-AU-BOIS (Map Hazebrouck 5a, Belgium; Square E, between RELY and AMETTES) Route taken from DROUVIN :- HESDIGNEUL, LABUISSIÈRE, PLACE A BRUAY, MARLES-LES-MINES, LOZINGHEM, AUCHEL, CAUCHY-A-LA-TOUR, FERFAY, BELLERY, AUCHY-AU-BOIS. (AUCHY-AU-BOIS is the new area in which the 81st Sanitary Section is billeted.)	Acting on instructions received from A.D.M.S. 16th Division. P.H.

Percival Hankey
Lieut RAMC.(T)
O.C. 81st Sanitary Section,

San: Sect: 81
Vol: 2.

(1st Division)
D/1. Dns

F/255/2.

Jan 1916

16

81 Sanitary Section
Jan
Vol

WAR DIARY
or
INTELLIGENCE SUMMARY.

(Erase heading not required.)

Army Form C. 2118.

Hour, Date, Place	Summary of Events and Information	Remarks and references to Appendices
8.30 Jan 1. 1916. p.m.	Left DROUVIN and proceeded with main body of my unit (advanced party having left on the 31.XII.15) to AUCHY-AU-BOIS, to new billets.	
11.0. Jan 2. 1916	Reported arrival in new billeting area to A.D.M.S. 16th Div PA	PA
Jan 10 1916	Examined water supply of AMETTES the new Headquarters of the 16th Division, and reported on the same	PA
Jan 13. 1916.	Investigated and reported upon a case of anopheles entering troops PA	
Jan 15. 1916	Interviewed O.C. 6th Mobile Laboratory (Hygiene) with reference to distribution of water for use of troops of 16th Division attached to my Headquarters.	PA
Jan 17. 1916.	Three disinfectors arrived for use of the 16th Division. Baths for the troops stationed at AMETTES & AMETTES of mines traced for 1st time on this day. An N.C.O. of my unit in charge of	PA
Jan 21. 1916.	Proceeded to FLECHINELLE to arrange with manager of mines there for baths for certain units of the 16th Division.	PA
Jan 23. 1916	Three disinfectors transferred from my Headquarters to 16th Divisional Laundry Depot	PA
Jan 26. 1916	To BETHUNE and interviewed O.C. 73rd Sanitary Section, 33rd Division	PA
Jan 28 1916	Commenced disinfection of underclothing discussed at the baths, in Thresh disinfector, at 16th Divisional Laundry Depot.	PA
Jan 1st 1916 to Jan 31 1916	Prepared an Monthly statistic in connection with the various units of the 16th Division	PA Percival Hartley Lieut

X 16th Div

81st Sany. Section

Feb 1916

Sau: Sect: 81
Vol: 3

War Diary
or
Intelligence Summary
of the
81st Sanitary Section
(16th Division)

16th Div.
"81st Sany Section

February   Volume 3

Army Form C. 2118.

Vol 3

WAR DIARY
or
INTELLIGENCE SUMMARY.
(Erase heading not required.)

Instructions regarding War Diaries and Intelligence Summaries are contained in F. S. Regs., Part II. and the Staff Manual respectively. Title pages will be prepared in manuscript.

Hour, Date, Place	Summary of Events and Information	Remarks and references to Appendices
Feb 1st 1916 – Feb 29th 1916	General. Routine inspection of billets, sanitary areas with supplies baths & laundries etc. Investigation of cases of measles in NEDONCHELLE and of diphtheria in ESTREE-BLANCHE. Disinfection of clothing, blankets and billets.	MH
Feb 27th 1916. 3 p.m.	Advance party of 5 men despatched to new billets at BUSNES.	MH
Feb 28th 1916. 9:45 a.m.	Main body left old billets at AUCHY-AU-BOIS and arrived at new billets at BUSNES at 11:30 a.m.	MH
12:0 n.n.	Reports arrival to A.D.M.S.	

Percival Huntley
Lieut (RAMC)
OC 81st Sanitary Section

WAR DIARIES

of

81st Sanitary Section- 16th Division

for the months of March and April 1916

COMMITTEE FOR THE
MEDICAL HISTORY OF THE WAR

Date   9 - JUN 1916

War Diary.
of the
81st Sanitary Section
16th Division

Volume 4 Sheets 1 + 2.

Army Form C. 2118.

Volume H / Sheet 11

WAR DIARY
or
INTELLIGENCE SUMMARY.
(Erase heading not required.)

Hour, Date, Place	Summary of Events and Information	Remarks and references to Appendices
March 1st to March 8th 1916.	My Headquarters were at BUSNES during this time. Engaged in the usual routine duties (sanitary) while here. A somewhat special feature was made of the examination of water supplies in the area, in accordance with instructions received from D.M.S. 1st Army (Letter No. P99/3, dated 24th Feb. 1916) Water supplies at BURNES, MIQUELLERIE, LE CORNET BOURDOIS, HAM-EN-ARTOIS, MANQUEVILLE, NORRENT FONTES, ST HILAIRE and BOURECQ were examined and tested. Report was submitted to ADMS 16th Division	M4
March 2nd March 9th 11-45 a.m.	Foden Disinfector arrived for the use of this Division from 2nd Division 81st Sanitary Section. Transport & Foden disinfector left billets at LILLERS BUSNES to proceed to new billets at LILLERS	M4 Acting under instructions from ADMS 16th Division
12-45 a.m.	Unit arrived at LILLERS. Arrival reported to ADMS.	M4
March 10th 1916 to March 26th 1916.	General Inspection of Billets, water supply, baths & of 16th Division. Construction latrines at MARLES-LES-MINES. Refuse latrines in LILLERS. Immediate cases of infectious disease among civilians in the area, disinfected premises &c, places premises out of bounds to troops & took necessary precautions to prevent the spread of disease. Investigated a case of SEPTICAEMIA (meningococcal) occurring in an officers billets. He contacts, disinfected billets, & placed billet out of bounds to troops.	M4
March 4th 1916	From disinfection transferred to 23rd Division, according to instructions from Medical 1st Corps (telegram m R 5 dated 17/3/16)	M4

Army Form C. 2118.
Volume 1
Sheet 7

WAR DIARY
or
INTELLIGENCE SUMMARY.
(Erase heading not required.)

Instructions regarding War Diaries and Intelligence Summaries are contained in F.S. Regs., Part II and the Staff Manual respectively. Title pages will be prepared in manuscript.

Hour, Date, Place	Summary of Events and Information	Remarks and references to Appendices
March 26th 1916.	Advance party proceeded to NOEUX-LES-MINES to take up billets in new area.	PH
March 27th 1916.	Main body of unit and transport left old billets at LILLERS and proceeded to new billets at NOEUX LES MINES	Acting under instructions from A.D.M.S. 16th Division. PH
1 p.m.	Arrived NOEUX-LES-MINES & reported arrival to A.D.M.S 16th Division. PH	
March 29th 1916.	Sent 6 men of the section to MAZINGARBE to arrange for their billets & return and instruct them as to their duties with regard to sanitation of MAZINGARBE & PHILOSOPHE.	PH
March 27th 1916 – 31st 1916.	Sanitary inspection of NOEUX-LES-MINES, MAZINGARBE, PHILOSOPHE, various trenches, and other parts of the area now occupied by this division.	PH

Percival Hartley
Captain RAMC
O.C. Sanitary Section

(73999) W4141—463. 400,000. 9/14. H.&J.Ltd. Forms/C. 2118/10.

Confidential

16 San
the "
Vol

War Diary
or
Intelligence Summary
of the
16th. Divisional Sanitary Section.
for
April 1916.

Volume 4.

Army Form C. 2118.

WAR DIARY
or
INTELLIGENCE SUMMARY.
(Erase heading not required.)

Hour, Date, Place	Summary of Events and Information	Remarks and references to Appendices
April 1st to April 30th 1916	During this month the 16th Divisional Sanitary Section has been stationed at NOEUX-LES-MINES, with the exception of a detachment at of six men at MAZINGARBE. Usual routine duties have been carried out, that is to say (I) Sanitary inspection of billeting areas, latrines &c. (II) Construction of, and repair to, latrines & urinals. (III) Disinfection of billets (IV) Supervision of manure removal (V) Examination of water supplies. (VI) Inspection of cases of infectious disease In addition experiments have been carried out on the Fly problem. Percival Hadley Capt RAMC T OC 16th San? Sect	

81 San Sec Vol 6

War Diary
or
Intelligence Summary
of the
81st. Sanitary Section
(16th. Division)

Vol. 6   Sheets 1 & 2

May 1916

COMMITTEE FOR THE
MEDICAL HISTORY OF THE WAR
Date 31 AUG. 1916

Army Form C. 2118.

WAR DIARY
or
INTELLIGENCE SUMMARY.
(Erase heading not required.)

Instructions regarding War Diaries and Intelligence Summaries are contained in F.S. Regs., Part II and the Staff Manual respectively. Title pages will be prepared in manuscript.

Hour, Date, Place	Summary of Events and Information	Remarks and references to Appendices
May 1st 1916 to May 31st 1916.	During this month the 81st Sanitary Section has been Stationed at NOEUX-LES-MINES, with the exception of a detachment of six men at MAZINGARBE. This detachment was increased to seven men on May 26th 1916. On May 1st the designation of this unit was changed to "16th Divisional Sanitary Section", but the old title was revived to on May 25th 1916, by orders received from A.D.M.S. 16th Division through D.M.S. 1st Army. Usual routine duties have been carried out: that is to say (i.) Sanitary inspection of billetting area; (latrines &c. (ii.) Construction of latrines, urinals, grease traps &c. (iii.) disinfection of billets (iv.) removal of manure (v.) examination of water supplies (vi.) investigation of cases of infectious disease. A scheme for the systematic removal of civilian refuse has been devised and put into operation in selected areas: this has been successful and it is proposed to adopt the system in other areas.	

Army Form C. 2118.

Vol 6/Sheet 7

WAR DIARY
or
INTELLIGENCE SUMMARY.
(Erase heading not required.)

Hour, Date, Place	Summary of Events and Information	Remarks and references to Appendices
	Several different types of fly-proof latrines have been constructed in the Sanitary Section workshop, and installed in different parts of the billetting area. Experiments on the efficacy of "C solution" and other substances in reducing the number of flies have been carried out and reports submitted to the A.D.M.S. 16th Division. I proceeded on leave to England on May 28th 1916 and returned on the expiration thereof. During my absence the duties of O.C. 81st Sanitary Section were performed by the D.A. D.M.S. 16th Division.	

Percival Hartley
Capt RAMC.
O.C. 81st Sanitary Section.

81 San Sec
Vol 7
June

Confidential

SANITARY SECTION
16th DIVISION

June 1916

War Diary

of

81st. Sanitary Section RAMC
(16th. Division)

June 1916.

Vol: 7. (Sheets 1 + 2)

Army Form C. 2118.

WAR DIARY
or
INTELLIGENCE SUMMARY.

(Erase heading not required.)

Instructions regarding War Diaries and Intelligence Summaries are contained in F. S. Regs., Part II. and the Staff Manual respectively. Title pages will be prepared in manuscript.

Hour, Date, Place	Summary of Events and Information	Remarks and references to Appendices
June 1/1916 to June 30th 1916.	During the month the 81st Sanitary Section has been stationed at NOEUX-LES-MINES with the exception of a detachment of seven men at MAZINGARBE. During the month the usual routine duties have been carried out. viz. (i) Sanitary inspection of billetting areas, latrine areas, horse lines, Camps, manure and refuse dumps, etc. (ii) Construction of a number of new "flyproof" latrines throughout the area. 25 of these have been constructed in the trenches. Repairs to existing latrines have also been carried out. (iii) New incinerators have been built at PHILOSOPHE and NOEUX-LES-MINES. Temporary "inable" incinerators have also been made of other oil drums and angle iron. All incineration one run in good repair. (iv) Disinfection of billets. (v) Removal of manure from civilian farm yards has been carried out in a number of farms briefly in NOEUX-LES-MINES and MAZINGARBE. (vi) Examination of water supplies. (vii) Investigation of cases of infectious diseases. (viii) Removal of civilian refuse. The refuse disposal has this month summary has been extended to other areas and is working satisfactorily.	

WAR DIARY
or
INTELLIGENCE SUMMARY.
(Erase heading not required.)

Army Form C. 2118.

Instructions regarding War Diaries and Intelligence Summaries are contained in F.S. Regs., Part II and the Staff Manual respectively. Title pages will be prepared in manuscript.

Hour, Date, Place	Summary of Events and Information	Remarks and references to Appendices
	(ix.) Sanitary inspection of civil lanes has been carried out and measures reported upon dealt with, either by the Sickness in cooperation with the civil authorities. Civilian refuse have been removed and cess-pits have been dealt with from time to time as necessity arose.	
	I returned from leave on June 7th and took over charge of the Section from D.A.D.M.S. 16th Division on the same and carried my duties during my absence.	
	I attended a conference of A.D.M.S. and O.C. Sanitary Sections of Division at Corps at BETHUNE on June 17th 1916. I have submitted reports on the following subjects during the week including the trenches occupied by units of the Division.	
	(i) Sanitary problem.	
	(ii) Report on the provision of latrines & transport for conservancy and other sanitary services in the billeting area.	OA.
	(iii) Report on Brew and Excreta in Billets for dealing with the measures taken in this respect for the various.	
	(iv) Report on Disinfection of fleas and lice infested pig-sties.	

P. Stratton R.M.C.
Capt.
O.C. 51st Sanitary Section.

WAR DIARY.

81st Sanitary Section

~~"A" AND "Q" BRANCH~~
~~HEADQUARTERS,~~
~~16TH. (IRISH) DIVISION~~

1st. July to 31st. July 1916.

VOLUME 8.

16

10th Division

81 p. Sany Section

July 1916

COMMITTEE FOR THE
MEDICAL HISTORY OF THE WAR
Date 5-SEP

Army Form C. 2118.

Vol. 8
Sheet 1

WAR DIARY
or
INTELLIGENCE SUMMARY.

(Erase heading not required.)

Instructions regarding War Diaries and Intelligence Summaries are contained in F.S. Regs., Part II and the Staff Manual respectively. Title pages will be prepared in manuscript.

Hour, Date, Place	Summary of Events and Information	Remarks and references to Appendices
July 1st 1916 to July 31st 1916	During the month the headquarters of the 87th Sanitary Section have remained at NOEUX-LES-MINES. A detachment of eight men have been billetted at MAZINGARBE during the month, for convenience as the work of these men is in the MAZINGARBE and PHILOSOPHE area. During the month 6 P.B. men have been transferred for duty (from the 20 P.B. men employed at MAZINGARBE) with the detachment at MAZINGARBE. The usual routine duties have been carried out during the month, viz:— (i.) Sanitary Inspection of Billetting areas. Ten NCOs and men were employed daily on these duties during the month. (ii.) Examination of water supplies. Two men from the unit specially trained in these duties were employed during the month. Inquiries regarding particular supplies in NOEUX-LES-MINES, Bois Hugo, PHILOSOPHE and a deaf dug out in 14 B 3.5 were investigated by me and reports and advice submitted. (iii.) Removal of civilian refuse proved regularly and without difficulty in NOEUX-LES-MINES. The club & mine P.B. men being used daily for the purpose, working under the direction of 1 NCO. of this unit. At MAZINGARBE two carts have been employed daily during the month. At PHILOSOPHE the removal of civilian refuse has proved a difficult matter.	

(73989) W41141—463. 400,000. 9/14. H.&J.Ltd. Forms/C. 2118/10.

WAR DIARY
or
INTELLIGENCE SUMMARY.
(Erase heading not required.)

Army Form C. 2118.

Vol 8
Sheet X

Hour, Date, Place	Summary of Events and Information	Remarks and references to Appendices

On account of the shortage of labour, I submitted a special report on this subject on July 13th 1916.

(IV) Manure from horse lines has been removed daily to the divisional manure dump. One NCO of this Labour has been in charge of the dump during the month, and has been assisted by 3. and sometimes 4 men.

(VI.) 5 cases of measles and 2 cases of para-typhoid disease.

Typhoid Fever: 13 have occurred in the Division. The usual measures were taken to trace the source and prevent the spread of infection. One case of Typhoid Fever in a civilian area notified by the French authorities. This was investigated and all necessary steps taken to prevent troops entering the lines and anyone using disinfection are warned as to disinfectants, supplies, instructions to soldiers and neighbours and to precautions to be taken. The case is under daily observation.

(VII) Constructional Works. 3 men of Section have been employed during the month in the workshop, in erecting sanitary appliances or conveniences where required. Two P.B. men are also employed in the workshop.

Different types of covers for deep fly proof trench latrines have been made and laid down in different

Army Form C. 2118.

Vol 8
Sheet 3

WAR DIARY
or
INTELLIGENCE SUMMARY.
(Erase heading not required.)

Hour, Date, Place	Summary of Events and Information	Remarks and references to Appendices

In the trenches 16 "half door" pattern loopholes have been found most suitable. 26 of this type, the majority having their tops down to the requisites bar loopholes, have been put down during the month in the LOOS sector and 18 in the 14 BIS sector. These were made in the 16½ Brs. in mid. workshop, on a plan and according to dimensions supplied by me. (Plan in steam opposite.) A strong framework of 2"×4" wood, 6' long by 4' wide was made covered with 16" planks, two in thus of which were tongued with a handle to serve as trap doors. They were taken up to the position in sections to pieces and the [ ] pits, dimensions of which were to be 5' long by 3' wide ones as possible, and covers for such [for] A number of different types of bins were issued. (stairs were also made and issued.) Wire mesh also made from time to time (hexcel or petrol) have been made in the workshop, and issued. A good many of the type shown in the drawing opposite have been issued and found satisfactory in practice.

Wire netting cages about 5 feet square, from [ ] kept, open at the top and at one side have been constructed near a number of incinerators to be acceptors of refuse pending its incineration. They have been found effective in curtailing the refuse and keeping the area tidy.

Army Form C. 2118.
Vol 8
Sheet 4

WAR DIARY
or
INTELLIGENCE SUMMARY.

(Erase heading not required.)

Hour, Date, Place	Summary of Events and Information	Remarks and references to Appendices
	About 300 "straight - wire fly-reins" Flycatchers have been made and issued during the month. Part of (them have been hung in) (strands. The wires are smeared with a viscous mixture of oil (2 pts) and resin (1 pt.) to which sugar or honey may be added. When covered with flies they are placed in the incinerators and then warmed and returned to their former position. They are very effective. A new type of incinerator, designed to burn faeces, has been completed during the month. It has been drawn & tried by Private J Scr of this section. A complete description & an account of its working will be submitted next month.	

Percival Hunter
Capt. RAMC
OC 91st Sanitary Section

Aug 1916

WAR DIARY.

81st Sanitary Section

MONTH OF AUGUST, 1916.

VOLUME :- 9.

COMMITTEE FOR THE
MEDICAL HISTORY OF THE WAR
Date 30 OCT. 1916

WAR DIARY
or
INTELLIGENCE SUMMARY.
(Erase heading not required.)

Army Form C. 2118.

Vol 9
Sheet 1

Hour, Date, Place	Summary of Events and Information	Remarks and references to Appendices
August 1st 1916 to August 31st 1916	**MOVEMENTS.** The head quarters of the 81st Sanitary Section remained at NOEUX-LES-MINES from Aug 1st to Aug 26th: a detachment of 8 men of the Section were posted for duty at MAZINGARBE and PHILOSOPHE and were billeted at MAZINGARBE. At 8 a.m. on Aug 26th the Section handed out of NOEUX-LES-MINES and arrived at MARLES-LES-MINES at 11.30 a.m. and billeted there until 7 p.m. August 29th, when the Section then marched to FOUQUEREUIL station where it arrived at 9 p.m., and entrained there. The train left FOUQUEREUIL at 12.10 a.m. on Aug 30th, and arrived at LONGEAU at 8.45 a.m. 30th August. The Section marched out of LONGEAU at 10.30 a.m. and proceeded to CORBIE where it arrived at 6 p.m. on Aug. 30th. The Section billeted at CORBIE for the night and left at 12 noon on August 31st and marched to the point L.2.B.o.9 (half MBERT, 1st Edition), known as "Forked Tree": the Section arrived here at 5 p.m. and occupied tents in the area occupied by 16th Divisional Head quarters. All movements were made according to orders issued by A.D.M.S. 16th Division. **Work** The state of the billeting area of the Division was inspected daily from Aug 1st to Aug 25th, (6 men of the Section being engaged on sanitary inspection during the period.) During	

WAR DIARY
or
INTELLIGENCE SUMMARY.
(Erase heading not required.)

Army Form C. 2118.

Volume 9
Sheet 2

Hour, Date, Place	Summary of Events and Information	Remarks and references to Appendices

13 The Division being in the rest, regular inspection and not be carried out during the half-six days of the month. These men were employed on the administering of latrines & in the disposal of refuse. The work was proceeded annually and was satisfactory carried out during the period. Two men were constantly engaged on water duties, examining the authorities supplies of pipeline network, and inspection of wells cuts and checking the chlorination of drinking water. These men were engaged in constructional work in Suction unhabited. Urine troughs and latrine seats were made and issued to various units of the Division. New latrines were constructed by the Section at PHILOSOPHE EAST (3) in NORTHERN UP PHILOSOPHE EAST (2) MAZINGARBE (2) WEST (2), MAZINGARBE (4) PERQUIN (3). New pits were made & minor pipes in MEUX-LES-MINES. Routine repairs to sanitary appliances were carried out by the Section where required in the area. Twenty latrine covers to fit over deep trench were made from biscuit boxes

Army Form C. 2118.

Volume 9
Sheet 3

WAR DIARY
or
INTELLIGENCE SUMMARY.
(Erase heading not required.)

Hour, Date, Place	Summary of Events and Information	Remarks and references to Appendices

With the avoidance of tactical spheres of fortification, sight of these were filled to a decent plan in the trenches, in the LOOS salient. The broken ground thereabout will be an obstacle and in the road and snow piled to fillers. An important advantage of this type of defense and is its easy transportability, one being able to carry it from the unhelp to the fire-bay where it is to be fixed. In the LOOS-HULLUCH sector this were an important factor in most of the long communication trenches to the distance of the fire and support trenches from the nearest trade billets. The system of spurs driftwork introduced in April 1916 in MOEUX LES MINES was maintained and works very late (actually these carts were used for the purpose in MOEUX - LENS - MINES) the two carts were sent to MAZINGARBE. Towards the end of the month the system (auxiliary that time — the him being empty far a several branch) was introduced into PHILOSOPHE EAST, and proved to be of great assistance in keeping the area in a clean condition. In PHILOSOPHE WEST the system broke down on account of the impossibility of securing labour to empty the barrels. In this area apreading has to be resorted to, on a greater extent than in other areas where the man ratio (actors

(73989) W4141—463. 400,000. 9/14. H.&J.Ltd. Forms/C. 2118/10.

Army Form C. 2118.

Volume 9
Sheet 4

WAR DIARY
or
INTELLIGENCE SUMMARY.
(Erase heading not required.)

Hour, Date, Place	Summary of Events and Information	Remarks and references to Appendices
immediate	Method of incineration was adopted. Manure from horse lines was removed regularly to the divisional dump. The area was maintained in a sanitary condition, and only 4 cases of infectious disease occurred during the month viz: 1 case of measles, 1 case of German measles, 1 case of scarlet fever, and one case of typhoid fever. So no fault of the divisional area. As flies appear in large numbers. They were numerous the last days, but nowhere did they become a nuisance or beyond control. I attribute this relative freedom from flies to the following measures which were adopted. (i.) Early in April the problem of refuse disposal from civil lines was taken in hand and the breeding places of flies destroyed. (ii.) The regulations for disposal of military refuse were enforced throughout the unit. This was effected by means of sanitary inspectors who made daily inspections and submitted daily reports to cover the whole area. The importance of removing refuse and destroying breeding places for flies was impressed on all ranks. (iii.) The removal of manure from horse lines was carried out daily. The majority of civilians were notices to cart their manure in to the lines, and kept after in to cart	

WAR DIARY
or
INTELLIGENCE SUMMARY.
(Erase heading not required.)

Army Form C. 2118.

Volume 9
Sheet 5

Hour, Date, Place	Summary of Events and Information	Remarks and references to Appendices

fiddling rules and dealt with training the Fly Vermin as N.C.O. of the unit, who speaks French fluently, has been detailed for dealing with civilian refuse, manure, cess-pits & latrines.

(ii) Active measures are taken from the start against the flies which have an early appearance. Among these measures may be mentioned:—

(i) Fly papers are used to make each in hay.
(ii) 70 "Swealain" Syringes for spraying refuse & manure heaps were issued to the Division.
(iii) 1200 fly traps were issued to the Division.
(iv) Fly catchers made of a straight piece of wire, bent at one end, and smeared with a nodel-castor oil mixture, were made in large numbers in Workshops & kept in latrines & other places frequented by flies.

I am of the opinion that the destruction of the early flies was an important factor in securing for the Division a relative immunity from this nuisance.

A new type of incinerator, designed for the incineration of faeces was used during the month, and was found to work satisfactorily. The principle of the incinerator is as follows. The incinerator is a square structure with a roof, containing a door for the reception of refuse. In no side there is a door.

WAR DIARY
or
INTELLIGENCE SUMMARY.
(Erase heading not required.)

Army Form C. 2118.

Volume 9
Sheet 6.

Instructions regarding War Diaries and Intelligence Summaries are contained in F.S. Regs., Part II and the Staff Manual respectively. Title pages will be prepared in manuscript.

Hour, Date, Place	Summary of Events and Information	Remarks and references to Appendices
	for removing burnt tins + into 4, sheeting of angle iron; 4 air shafts, one in centre of each side + at the bottom. Built into the centre of the incinerator is an oblong cage or chamber made of angle iron at the 4 bottom, thin rods on the angle iron grating; at the top it communicates with a hopper made of a lantern panel with the bottom removed. The hopper is built into the roof and the top of the hopper can be closed with a lid. A chimney and flue is also provided, and an opening is left in the chimney (inside the incinerator) near the top of the angle iron cage; this ensures a strong draught inside the cage itself. A fire is made inside the incinerator; faeces are added through the hopper and pass into the cage, where they are dried and then burnt. The ashes drop out of the cage into the incinerator pit. The cage requires occasional stoking. This type of incinerator possesses a good many advantages; viz:- (i) fuel used is generated, and all the tins + is made use of. (ii) The faeces are subjected to the great heat + thoroughly dried. Subsequent incineration is relatively easy. (iii) Once the faeces have been passed down the hopper into the cage they cannot be removed. They must first be reduced to ashes. (iv) No smell was observed during incineration of faeces, so long as a good fire was maintained in the incinerator.	This incinerator was designed and constructed by A/Cpl J.J. BOX 81st Sanitary Section

Army Form C. 2118.

1869
Sheet 4.

WAR DIARY
or
INTELLIGENCE SUMMARY.
(Erase heading not required.)

Instructions regarding War Diaries and Intelligence Summaries are contained in F.S. Regs., Part II. and the Staff Manual respectively. Title pages will be prepared in manuscript.

Hour, Date, Place	Summary of Events and Information	Remarks and references to Appendices

During the month special reports were submitted to A.D.M.S. 16th Division dealing with the following subjects:—

(1.) Report on the billets in PHILOSOPHE WEST with recommendations as to the necessary improvements to be carried out to take same more habitable during the approaching cold weather. (These improvements were in course of being carried out when the Division moved from the area.)

(2.) Report on the water supplies of VERMELLES.

(3.) Report on the water supply of PHILOSOPHE KEEP.

(4.) Report on the effect of exposure of lice eggs to an atmosphere containing 3% sulphur dioxide, such as is produced by burning sulphur in a closed room.

P.H.

Percival Hunter
Capt. RAMC (T.)
OC 81st Sanitary Section.

Sept 1916

WAR DIARY

81st Sanitary Section RAMC

FOR MONTH OF SEPTEMBER, 1916.

VOLUME 10

Army Form C. 2118.

Volume 10
Sheet 1

WAR DIARY
or
INTELLIGENCE SUMMARY.
(Erase heading not required.)

Instructions regarding War Diaries and Intelligence Summaries are contained in F. S. Regs., Part II. and the Staff Manual respectively. Title pages will be prepared in manuscript.

Hour, Date, Place	Summary of Events and Information	Remarks and references to Appendices
Sep. 1st to Sep. 30th 1916.	MOVEMENTS. The Headquarters of the 819 Infantry & others remained at FORKED TREE camp [L.2.b.1.9.] from Aug 31st 1916 to Sep 5th 1916. At 7.0 a.m Sep 5th 1916 an advance party of the unit proceeded to the Citadel Camp [J.21 Central] and the whole unit has arrived in there new quarters at 9 a.m. On Sep 7th 1916 the Headquarters the unit moved to another part of the CITADEL camp [J.21.C.6.5.] where it remained until 10th Sep 1916. The unit then removed to the original camp at the CITADEL [J.21.Central] and on the following day, Sep 11th 1916, at 10 a.m., the unit marched to CORBIE and arrived there at 6 P.m. On Sep 18th 1916 the unit left CORBIE and marched to LA NEUVILLE and was conveyed from here by motor bus to AIRAINES, arriving there at 9 p.m on 18th Sep. 1916. On 21st Sep 1916, the unit L/E AIRAINES at 7 p.m and marched to LONG PRÉ where it arrived at 9 p.m. and entrained at once. The unit detrained on the following day, 22nd Sep 1916, at GODEWAERSVELDE [MAP 27 France Philippine Q.18.b.2.9.] at 9.0 a.m and marched to WESTOUTRE [MAP 28 M.9.c.6.1] where it arrived at 12 noon.	hqs. — ALBERT 1st EST

Army Form C. 2118.

WAR DIARY
or
INTELLIGENCE SUMMARY.
(Erase heading not required.)

Hour, Date, Place	Summary of Events and Information	Remarks and references to Appendices
	Work. At FORKED TREE camp, energetic measures were taken to deal with the fly nuisance. Flies were encountered here in great numbers. A number of large messes were situated in the camp, it was difficult to prevent sick flies. It was found that spraying the latrines and canvas huts with creosote kept flies away. It was found necessary to spray the latrines twice daily, and to keep the flaps closed during the day. Fly wires covered with oil were hung up in the tents & huts and did good service. The whole camp was cleared of refuse which was burnt, and areas which had been fouled with old faeces as tins &c, and on which flies swarmed, were also sprayed. A new latrine was made in the camp. Similar measures were adopted in 2 adjoining camps with fair success. The number of flies being considerably reduced. The sanitary inspection of the camp was carried out during our stay, and anti-fly corpses were detailed for duty at the breeding water stations. A number of cesspits latrine areas were had + burned now to the morning to burn. At the Citadel the work against flies no details about were	

Army Form C. 2118.
Volume 10
Sheet 3

WAR DIARY
or
INTELLIGENCE SUMMARY.
(Erase heading not required.)

Hour, Date, Place	Summary of Events and Information	Remarks and references to Appendices
	Continued. An advanced sub section of 10 NCOs then was established at CARNOY [MAP ref. A 13 b.] Sanitary inspection of this area was carried out; these incinerators were made of ample iron in CARNOY and the billeting area (which necessitates an infantry brigade) was cleared of a good deal of refuse. Four new latrines were constructed (deep trench, with fly proof covers) and repairs to existing latrines carried out. These which were made at CARNOY. I had an enquiry into the water supply of this area and water duty corporals were posted at the filling places. A new incinerator was made in the CITADEL CAMP, and one latrine was demolished and a new one constructed in its place. At CORBIE, I interviewed the Town Major and the Town Sanitary Officer. The Sanitary areas at CORBIE were found to be in a bad state of repair, and in a dirty condition. Three refusing latrines were found from the Section and 2 or 3 T.U. new atlaches to each. They were provided with tools and material and very necessary repairs to latrines &	

WAR DIARY
INTELLIGENCE SUMMARY.
(Erase heading not required.)

Army Form C. 2118.

Volume 10

Hour, Date, Place	Summary of Events and Information	Remarks and references to Appendices

Incinerators carried out. A new incinerator was made for the use of Headquarters. Six new urinals were made at CORBIE. Sanitary inspectors of the billets in CORBIE, SAILLY LE SEC and VAUX-SUR-SOMME were carried out. At the billets named places practically no sanitary conveniences existed at all. I interviewed the Town Major on the matter and made a survey of these two villages, and submitted written recommendations for central sanitary areas. Reports were duly submitted [RS1 & RS2] through A Dns 16th Division, dealing with the creation of these 2 villages, and forwarding to Town Major's SAILLY-LE-SEC: the decision arrived at of the area before the work could be taken in hand. An examination of the water supplies of the CORBIE – VAUX – SAILLY-LE-SEC area was carried out, the best outfalls being labelled for the filling of water carts & the amount of bleaching powder required for sterilisation of the water stated on a notice fixed to each supply. Notices showing the situation ... were made & fixed in CORBIE.

Army Form C. 2118.

Volume 10
Sheet 5.

WAR DIARY
or
INTELLIGENCE SUMMARY.
(Erase heading not required.)

Hour, Date, Place	Summary of Events and Information	Remarks and references to Appendices

The unit has been in the WESTOUTRE – LOCRE – LA CLYTTE – KEMMEL area for the last week of this month. Four N.C.O's from this unit working with 9 attached T.O. men, have been put at LOCRE: 2 Inspectors and KEMMEL & Locally, and 2 Inspectors are working h. WESTOUTRE. A careful enquiry has been made into the question of the water supply in this area. I interviewed the O.C. IR Corps Water Patrols immediate on arrival in this area and ascertained from him the situation of all (water borehole) Stations, and Reservoir & catchment areas. This same orderlies was posts at each borehole Water Stations, to ensure correct chlorination of all borehole Water, Steamers of Tanks, carts etc. a Return from this unit gets the supplies at each station daily, and the quantity of bleaching powder required each day, is posted on a Notice Board at each Station. Records are also kept of all carts filling at the various stations, the condition of the carts, bleaching powder etc.

Latrines and urinals in this area have been visited daily. Necessary repairs to these structures are being carried out, and new latrine trough traps have been made in the workshop and constructed when required.

Percival Hathway Capt. R.A.M.C.T.
O.C. 51st Sanitary Section

WAR DIARY

MONTH OF OCTOBER, 1916.

VOLUME

81st Sanitary Section

Army Form C. 2118.

VOL XI
SHEET 1.

WAR DIARY
or
INTELLIGENCE SUMMARY.
(Erase heading not required.)

Hour, Date, Place	Summary of Events and Information	Remarks and references to Appendices
Oct 1st 1916 to Oct 31st 1916	Movements & disposition of Section. The headquarters of the Section remained at HOSTOUTRE during the month. 14 men of the wind were posted for duty at LOCRE, one team at NIPPENHOEK. Six men were engaged on sanitary inspection duty in all parts of the area and remainder at Headquarters for Water Intaine. Four men were posts for duty at different brewery water Stations and 14 R.A.M.C. privates from the trained Field Ambulance were attached for duty in connection with breaking Water Bottles. Four men were employed on constructional work both in the workshops & in the Divisional Area. Work. Arrangements made for the control of breaking water supplies proved satisfactory during the month. The water tanks are cleaned regularly once a week. An improvement in the quality of the breaking water has been noted during the month & this is due in part to the attention which has been given to the storage tanks, and partly to the attention which has been	

Army Form C. 2118.

VOL XI
SHEET. 2.

WAR DIARY
or
INTELLIGENCE SUMMARY.
(Erase heading not required.)

Hour, Date, Place	Summary of Events and Information	Remarks and references to Appendices
	given to the filling and the reservoirs. A suggestion was made to the Tr Corps that tank shells might be manufactured of sufficient at KEMMEL SHELTERS and these sometimes of sufficient size to hold petrol which he drew from the L. of C. details. Finally, if drawn up a circular dealing with the later supplies in the time and acts showing how beaten, stating the rules to be observed for the filling of carts, the care of carts, stacking promptly re... (then were circulated to all ranks in the Division. A copy is attached Q 23/8 proposal of human excreta. Attention of the troops in some drawn to the important matter by the IX Corps who the necessity for burning all faeces was emphasized and reports on the subject ...K.157 and 16th Division and ...alemates for the approved new type of movement ... constructed for the purpose of incineration of faeces .... ..elements announced to attend to this amalgamation dealing with the subject, and this ...many together with ... showing the type of incinerator to be constructed was circulated to all units in the Division	

WAR DIARY or INTELLIGENCE SUMMARY

Army Form C. 2118.

Vol. XI
SHEET 3

Summary of Events and Information

In consultation with O.R.E. 16th Division in a type of latrine was decided upon for use in the Division. 96 is of proof, trenches will have been fastening trench boards for any straining and arranging so that the mine & faces are on afterwards; the mine is run direct into a soakage pit to the faces are collected in buckets & taken away somewhat. The bucket contents are burnt in the incinerator. A drawing of the latrine was prepared for reference & guidance. A copy is attached.   A 13/9

9 Last advised as to the site, for sanitary arrangements in camps. These have been attended to as far as possible.

Sanitary inspection of the area has been carried out one the inspection has received attention in the construction of latrines and incinerators. Great care was now being paid to the building of incinerators & the construction of latrines & urinals.

Percival Stanley Rowan
Capt. R.A.M.C.
O.C. 81st Sanitary Section
16th Division

Q.23/8.

DRINKING WATER SUPPLIES IN THE 16TH. DIVISIONAL AREA.

1. The following DRINKING WATER STATIONS are available for the use of the troops of the Division:-
    (a) No.24 at WESTOUTRE (M.9.c. 8.1)
    (b) No.36 at WESTOUTRE (M.9.d. 2.2)
    (c) No.37 on the main road from CANADA CORNER to LACLYTE (M.12.d. 2.3).
    (d) No.21 on the LA CLYTE - KEMMEL road (N.13.b. 9.7).
    (e) No.22 on the LA CLYTE - BRULOOZE Road (N.13.a. 5.5).
    (f) No.25 on the LOCRE - BAILLEUL Road (M.34.a. 9.8).
    (g) No.23 at KEMMEL SHELTERS (N.20.c. 1.2).

At stations Nos.22 and 24.there are arrangements for the filling of carts only. At the remaining stations there are in addition to the arrangements for filling water carts, facilities for filling water bottles, petrol tins and camp kettles. At station No.23 only one cart at a time can be filled, and there is at present only one tank for the filling of water bottles, petrol tins, and camp kettles.

2. In addition to the above there is a piped supply to the right sector, and part of the centre sector of the trenches. This is drawn from storage tanks situated on MONT KEMMEL. The water in the tanks is treated with the requisite quantity of cloride of lime, before being conveyed to the trenches by pipes. There are stand pipes situated in N.23.d., N.23.a., N.28.b., N.29.a., and N.29.b.

3. The following measures have been adopted to ensure a safe supply of drinking water for troops:-
    (a) The water at each station is tested daily by a N.C.O.of the 81st.Sanitary Section. The amount of bleaching powder required per water cart is determined, and the figure posted on the notice board fixed at each station.
    (b) R.A.M.C.Orderlies are posted at each station. They will personally see that the requisite amount of bleaching powder, as determined for the day, is added to each water cart before it leaves the station. They will inspect the carts, the condition of the bleaching powder, and will keep a record of all carts filling at their respective stations.
    (c) At those stations where facilities are afforded for the filling of water bottles, petrol tins and camp kettles, the water in the tanks specially set apart for this purpose is chlorinated by the R.A.M.C.Orderlies attached to the station. They will be informed daily, at the time of the test, of the amount of bleaching powder which is to be added to each tank.
    (d) A stock (about 12) of $\frac{1}{4}$ lb.tins of bleaching powder (chloride of lime) is to be kept in a dry place in all Quartermaster's Stores and issued to water carts as required. Each cart should invariably carry two such tins, one in use, and one in reserve. No tin should be used for more than 5 days, as frequent opening of the tin results in the powder becoming moist, with consequent deterioration of its sterilising power. All water carts should be provided with a vessel preferably of enamel ware in which the emulsion of bleaching powder is prepared, prior to its addition to the water cart.

(Sd). W.B.Rennie. Captain.
for Lieut Colonel.
A.A.& Q.M.G., 16th.Division.

1st October 1916.

16th DIV.No.A.13/9.

SANITATION.

Owing to the ~~~~~ nature of the soil, the sources of the drinking water supplies and the occurrence of a considerable number of cases of Dysentery in the Division, the question of sanitation generally, and the disposal of human excreta in particular, is one of extreme importance.

It has been decided that incineration is the only safe method of dealing with excreta and an order to this effect has been issued by the Army. In order to carry this out, it is necessary that the latrine, the urine soakage pit, and the incinerator should be grouped together.

Latrines:- should be of the bucket type. They should be provided with canvas screens, corrugated iron roof and fly proof seats on the plan usually provided by the R.E. A trough should be fixed on the edge of the seat to conduct the urine direct into the urine soakage pit. Sawdust should be placed in the latrine buckets.

Urine Soakage Pit:- The usual type consists of a large square hole in the ground, filled with burnt tins and stones, or bricks, large ones at the bottom, smaller ones over these, and a layer of stones at the top. Each pit has a trough made of biscuit tins or oil drums leading into it.

Incinerators:- must be constructed so as to consume both rubbish and faeces. Three types are shewn on the attached sketches.

Type C:- The drawing and following description are supplied by D.D.M.S., IX Corps:-

"The incinerator is built of oil or biscuit tins filled with mud. It has a closed top and two corrugated iron shelves. The upper one for faeces and the lower one for rubbish. The open front can be closed when it is in action by a sheet of corrugated iron with a hole cut in the bottom leaving a sufficient space to create a draught."

A chimney should be constructed in a similar way as shewn in Type "A".

Type "A":- The drawings shewn have been made from an incinerator constructed by the 11th Hants in their camp at M.12.c.5.2; it may be seen there. Made according to the dimensions shewn, it is capable of burning the rubbish and excreta from a camp of 1,000 to 1,200 men.

Materials required: 1,800 bricks, 30 pieces of 5'.6" rivetting angle iron, three pieces of strong corrugated iron, 1 oil drum to serve as chimney pot, and 3 covers or doors which can be made of corrugated iron.

The walls are 9" thick: the roof, containing two apertures as shewn, is supported on angle iron. Excreta is added through the smaller aperture near the chimney on to the 2' corrugated iron plate where it is first dried, and then burnt. Refuse is added through the larger aperture in the roof and the fire is stoked through the door at the front.

Type "B":- is constructed on a somewhat different principle. There is a central rectangular cage or chamber made of angle iron, the lower end of which rests on the grating and the upper end communicates with a hopper (H. on sketch), made from a latrine pail with the bottom removed. Latrine buckets are emptied into the hopper and the contents pass into the vertical iron cage where they are dried and then burnt. Refuse is added at the door shewn on the slope and the fire is stoked from the door at the front. The drawing shows an incinerator of this type constructed to burn refuse and excreta from a camp of 1,000 to 1,200 men.

Materials required:-

P. T. O.

Materials required: 1,505 bricks, 40 pieces of 3'.6" rivetting angle iron, 1 latrine pail, 4 oil drums (chimney) 3 covers or doors which can be made from corrugated iron. Further details as to the construction of this type of incinerator can be had from Officer Commanding, 81st Sanitary Section, who can also provide angle iron cages. An incinerator of this type (full size) has been constructed at 112th Field Ambulance at WESTOUTRE, and may be seen there.

In all camps and billeting areas as yet unprovided with incinerators for burning excreta, steps should be taken at once to construct one of appropriate size in the sanitary area.

Officer Commanding Sanitary Section, will give every assistance and advice in regard to the siting and construction of these incinerators and is preparing a scheme for joint plants in the case of areas where several units are in close proximity.

The incinerators require constant supervision by the men of the sanitary squads of units. As pointed out in the IX Corps circular on this subject, one of the principal requirements for success is a slight degree of industry and intelligence in supervision. As every Infantry Battalion has its sanitary cadre of 8 men who do nothing but sanitation, and every other unit is supplied with like proportion, there should be no difficulty in carrying out rigid supervision of latrines and incinerators.

Second Army Routine Order No. 230 dated 4.11.15, authorises the issue of additional pay at the rate of 8d. a day for men working at the incinerator of excreta and refuse on the following scales:-

For incinerators burning excreta and refuse for units)
from 100 to 500 men...........................) one man.
For incinerators burning excreta and refuse for units)
from 500 to 1,200 men..........................) two men.
(Authority D.A.G., 3rd Echelon, 10918,"B", dated 30.10.15).

It is hoped that the stimulus of this extra duty pay combined with careful supervision will ensure the necessary degree of efficiency in this work on which the health of the troops so largely depends.

R. B. Rennie Capt
for
. Lieut-Colonel,
A.A.& Q.M.G., 16th Division.

14th October, 1916.

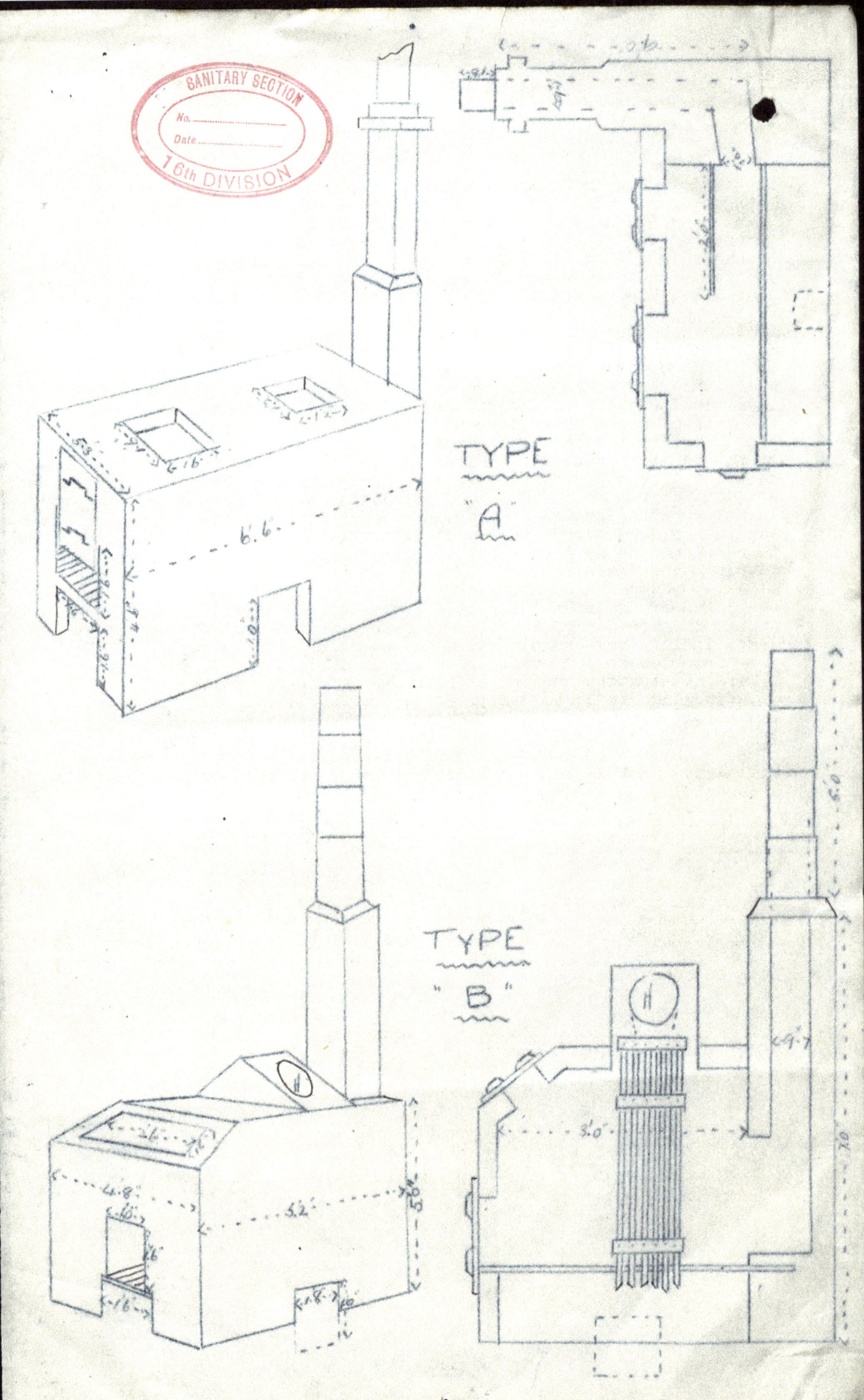

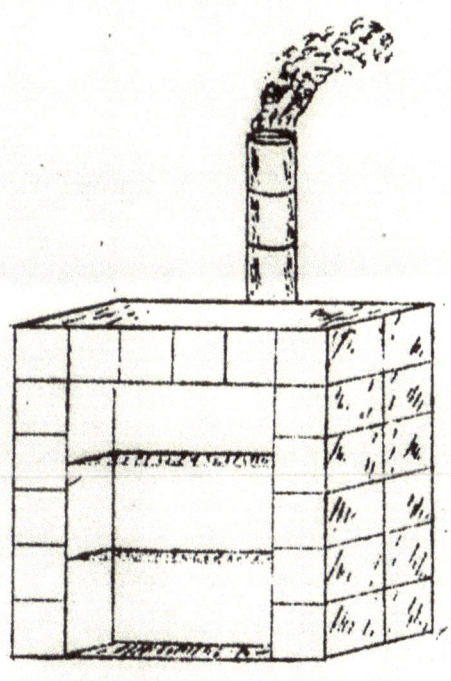

TYPE "C"

INCINERATOR

MEN'S LATRINE

Scale: $\frac{1}{2}$" = 1 foot

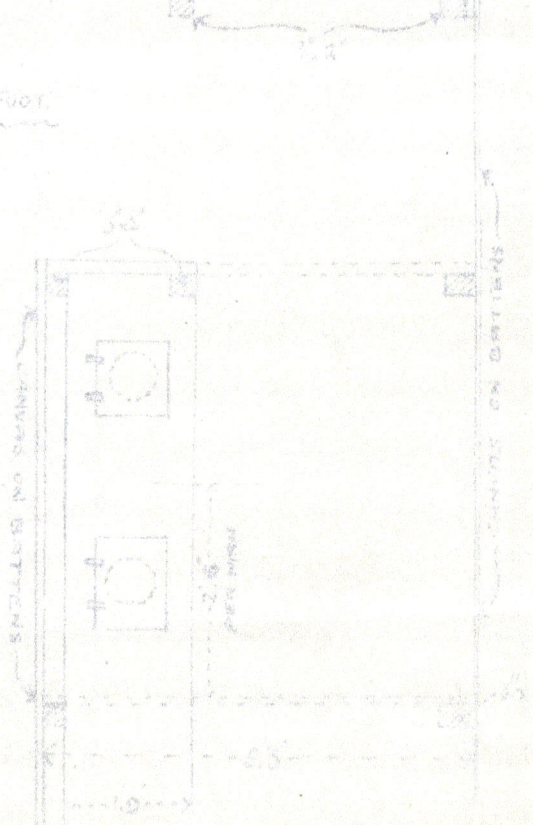

NOTE.
Seat & back flaps
hinged with leather
or canvas.
Inclined trough in
front of latrine
boxes connected
to sump.

WAR DIARY.

FOR

MONTH OF NOVEMBER, 1916.

VOLUME 12.

81st Sanitary Section R.A.M.C.

Army Form C. 2118.

VOL XII
SHEET 1

WAR DIARY
INTELLIGENCE SUMMARY

Place	Date	Hour	Summary of Events and Information	Remarks and references to Appendices
WESTOUTRE	1/6 to 30/6		During the month of November the Sanitary Section has been stationed at WESTOUTRE with the exception of 4 men posted at LOCRE. The following routine duties have been carried out during the month. 1) Sanitary Inspections of Camps, billeting area, latrine area, horse lines, manure & refuse dumps &c. 2) A large number of new incinerators have been constructed & the area generally adapted for the burning of rubbish, refuse, & litter. 3) Dry pail latrines with fixed sun-bleach boxes and good standing have been erected in practically all Camps and billeting areas. 4) Baths have been inspected when necessary. All the drinking water supplies in the Divisional Area are under the control of this Section. The tanks are systematically cleaned and no water is allowed to be used without being properly chlorinated.	

Army Form C. 2118.

VOL XII
SHEET II

WAR DIARY
or
INTELLIGENCE SUMMARY.
(Erase heading not required.)

Place	Date	Hour	Summary of Events and Information	Remarks and references to Appendices
			1. A Conservancy system has been established for the two principal villages in the Area vis: WESTOUTRE & LOCRE under the supervision of two N.C.Os belonging to the section, whereby all excreta urine is collected daily & taken to incinerators and burnt. The system is working satisfactorily. 2. The practice of maintaining workshops has been continued and a large number of box latrine seats, urine troughs, urinals, grease traps &c have been sent out to different units. 3. Recommendations re improving advanced units supply at Kemmel was submitted to A.D.M.S. 16th Divi. Copy A attached. OC Section (Capt D. Hartley Raine) was admitted to Field Ambulance sick on 15th inst. and the duties have been performed by D.A.D.M.S. 16th Divi. Lt D.A.D.M.S. (Sanitation) 2nd Army held a conference of D.A.D's M.S. + O.S.C. Sanitary Sections re organization & duties of Sanitary Sections on 14/6.	

H. G. Sheehen
Major RAMC
for O.C. 81st Sanitary Section

"A"

A.D.M.S.,
   16th.Division.

    Attached is a plan of the Water Tanks on KEMMEL HILL at present and as proposed.

    In 1. it will be seen that both pipes from the filter tank enter one of the storage tanks which is connected with the other by a pipe near the bottom, and it will be observed that the water from both tanks is always flowing which makes proper chlorination practically impossible. Some of the water might be short of chlorine and on the other hand if only a small amount is used in the trenches, the water is apt to be over chlorinated.

    In 2. it will be seen that the pipes are so arranged, with the necessary valves, to shut off either tank, and by this means a proper system of chlorination is obtained.

    A small tank with the necessary valves is also shown for mixing and delivery of Bleaching Powder Solution.

G.F.Sheehan.

Major, RAMC,
for O.C., 81st. Sanitary Section.

SANITARY SECTION — 16th DIVISION
No. D.70
Date 22/11/1916.

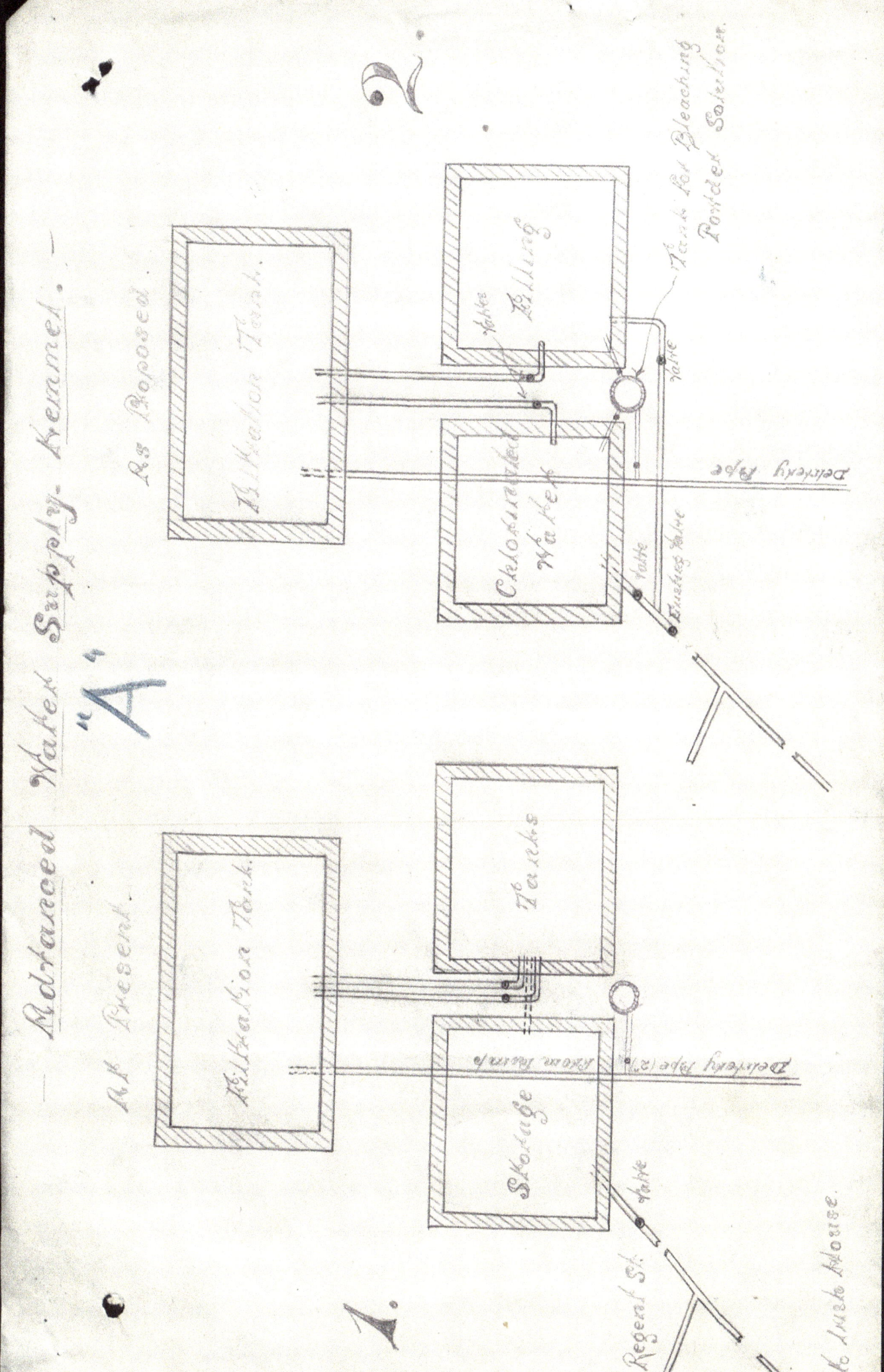

WAR DIARY FOR MONTH OF DECEMBER, 1916.

VOLUME 13

R.A.M.C. 81st Sanitary Section

COMMITTEE FOR THE
MEDICAL HISTORY OF THE WAR
Date 31 JAN. 1917

Army Form C. 2118.

Vol-XIII
Sheet 1.

WAR DIARY
INTELLIGENCE SUMMARY.
(Erase heading not required.)

Place	Date	Hour	Summary of Events and Information	Remarks and references to Appendices
In the field	Dec 1st 1916 to Dec 31st 1916		The Headquarters of the 81st Sanitary Section remained at WESTOUTRE during the month, a subsection being stationed at LOCRE. The strength of the subsection varies according to the requirements of the work to be done and numbered 10 on Dec 31st 1916. There men of the unit were engaged on water duties during the month. A workshop has been established with the advanced subsection at LOCRE to deal with the work in that and the KEMMEL area & the Headquarters workshop (2 men employed) still being maintained. Water Supplies. Ten "P.B." men have been posted for duty at the hotels, Inns &c in the area relieving R.A.M.C. personnel from Field Ambulances who have been engaged a few tests and have now been returned to the Headquarters of their units. Structural alteration to the piping at the reservoirs in MONT KEMMEL have been carried out during the month, whereby the tanks can be used in alternate charge and the process of sterilization & distribution of water to the troops has been considerably simplified. Repairs to the supply to the troughs have been carried out. The water station was closed during the month (No. 22) as it was little used and another tank was available & conveniently run. The work of bending the pipe on a set-up and	

2353 Wt. W2344/1454 700,000 5/15 D. D. & L. A.D.S.S./Forms/C. 2118.

WAR DIARY or INTELLIGENCE SUMMARY

Army Form C. 2118.

Vol XIII
SHEET 2.

against frost has been begun. The quality of the water has remained good. The waterworks supplying the reserves at WHITE CHATEAU, LOCRE has been patrolled with a view to discovering possible sources of pollution.

Construction of H.N.R. — has been told off a little on account of shortage of material during the month. Six incinerators were completed during the month, two of them being of new pattern designs for adaptation to drying areas; pattern mine troughs of various sizes were constructed and fixed up in different parts of the Divisional area; two grease traps were made in different camps. New latrines were constructed in 1 camp at HESTOUTRE and in 2 camps at LOCRE. Repairs to latrines were carried out at PERRY HUTS. Hand baths, improvised from 4 gallon petrol tins, were made in the workshop and issued to units on samples. The first this was constructed by the Section during the month.

General. Difficulties in the disposal of urine by soakage from camps arose during the month. This was reported upon by the E. ADMS 16th Division and recommendations for dealing with the problem were made. The cooperation of the R.E's has been obtained and work is now in progress.

Army Form C. 2118.

VOL XIII
SHEET 3

WAR DIARY
or
INTELLIGENCE SUMMARY.
(Erase heading not required.)

Instructions regarding War Diaries and Intelligence Summaries are contained in F. S. Regs., Part II. and the Staff Manual respectively. Title pages will be prepared in manuscript.

Place	Date	Hour	Summary of Events and Information	Remarks and references to Appendices
			During the month reports on the sanitary condition of CURRAGH CAMP, and recommendations for the improvement of latrines stoves and latrines of BIRR BARRACKS were submitted to A.D.M.S. XVIth Division. New huts have been erected at BUTTERFLY FARM, BIRR BARRACKS, DERRY HUTS and in several smaller camps in the area. O.C. 81st Sanitary Section lectured at the 16th Divisional School on Dec 13th 1916 on Field Sanitation, and attended a meeting of the IX Corps Medical Board on Dec 26th.16. PM.	

Percival Hunter
Capt. R.A.M.C.T.
O.C. 81st Sanitary Section.

WAR DIARY for month of JANUARY, 1917.

VOLUME 14

RAMC 81st Sanitary Section

16th Div.

Jan. 1917

Vol 14

COMMITTEE FOR THE
MEDICAL HISTORY OF THE WAR
Date 13 MAR 1917

WAR DIARY
INTELLIGENCE SUMMARY.

Army Form C. 2118.
Vol. XIV
Sheet

Place	Date	Hour	Summary of Events and Information	Remarks and references to Appendices
In the Field	Jan 1st 1917 to Jan 31st 1917		The Headquarters of the 81st Sanitary Section remained at WESTOUTRE during the month, a subsection of 10 men being maintained at LOCRE. These men of the unit were engaged in their duties. A workshop has been established at LOCRE with the subsection there, and has proved useful in making various Sanitary appliances required at KEMMEL and LOCRE. The workshop at headquarters has been maintained as usual during the month. Water Supplies. During the latter half of the month difficulties arose with regard to the Supplies of drinking water, on account of severe frost. Prompt measures were taken to deal with the situation, with the result that with the exception of a few hours on the morning of Jan 24 a constant supply of drinking water has been available for troops billeted in the area. During the month a sub cart has been detailed and a water duty newly appointed to supply several small units billetted in KEMMEL VILLAGE. The situation of IX Corps Water Point was drawn - on Jan 18th and again on Jan 30th - to the dangerous condition of the Platform at Strombeke Water Station No. 25 at LOCRE. This is a most urgent and serious matter. Three letters have been written caused by motor lorries carrying large water tanks on board and no steps have yet on the subject since Dec 12th 1916, but no reply has been received and no steps have yet been taken to alter the matter. A report was submitted through ADMS. 16th Division	

Army Form C. 2118.

Vol XIV
Sheet 2

WAR DIARY
or
INTELLIGENCE SUMMARY.
(Erase heading not required.)

Instructions regarding War Diaries and Intelligence Summaries are contained in F. S. Regs., Part II. and the Staff Manual respectively. Title pages will be prepared in manuscript.

Place	Date	Hour	Summary of Events and Information	Remarks and references to Appendices
			To President II Corps Note Boards on the possible sources of pollution of the reservoir and catchment at WHITE CHATEAU, LOCRE. (Jan 2nd 1917)	
			Constructional Work. Shortage of material and inclement weather have interfered somewhat with the constructional work carried out by the section. The following is a summary of the new work completed during the month.	
			(a) 3 Box-seat fly proof latrines, various types, constructed in the workshop and erected in the Camps of the 16th SAC, 77th Brigade RFA, and DERRY HUTS.	
			(b) The following work has been done in KEMMEL VILLAGE	
			(i) 3 large latrines, 1 for the 49th MGC and 2 for public use have been erected at convenient sites in the village	
			(ii) 1 large brick incinerator, plate type, erected near the lines of the 49th M.G.C.	
			(iii) 3 urinals	
			(iv) 2 grease traps	
			(v) Fifteen Standing the victualling of the sanitary area in the village made and erected.	
			(During the month a sanitary man has been appointed at KEMMEL VILLAGE; he has provided a cellar in which watering can be stored confortarily, and his appointment + help	

WAR DIARY
or
INTELLIGENCE SUMMARY.
(Erase heading not required.)

Army Form C. 2118.

Vol XIV
Sheet 3.

Place	Date	Hour	Summary of Events and Information	Remarks and references to Appendices
			in this and other ways have been of great help in carrying out the work in this village.)	
			(c) Two grease traps and hutes in camps at LOCRE	
			(d) Urinals made in the workshop and erected in camps out of the 7th Royal Irish Rifles and the canteen at KEMMEL SHELTERS	
			(e) Refuse receptacles made in the workshop and supplies to Y.M.C.A. hut, KEMMEL SHELTERS and 16th Divisional Headquarters.	
			(f) An incinerator for the burning of civilian refuse erected at LOCRE	
			General. (i) Trials and experiments as to the efficacy of the disinfector work which is being carried out at the trimmer laundry; a report was submitted to A.D.M.S 16th Division on Jan 6th	PA
			(ii) I lectures at the Corps School of Sanitation on Jan 25th in the carriage of disposal.	
			(iii) I attended conferences of O.C. Sanitary Sections, 2nd Army on Jan 28th and Jan 31st at 2nd Army Headquarters.	

Percival Hewlett
Capt RAMC
O.C. 81st Sanitary Section

WAR DIARY.

FOR MONTH OF FEBRUARY, 1917.

VOLUME 15

UNIT:- 81st Sanitary Section
R.A.M.C.

Army Form C. 2118.

Vol. XV
Sheet 1

WAR DIARY
INTELLIGENCE SUMMARY.
(Erase heading not required.)

Place	Date	Hour	Summary of Events and Information	Remarks and references to Appendices
In the Field	Feb 1st to Feb 28th 1917		**LOCATION and MOVEMENTS.** The headquarters of the 87th Sanitary Section remained at WESTOUTRE during the month. A sub section of 10 men being maintained at LOCRE. 3 men of the unit were engaged on duties in connection with water supply. One corporal and 9 men is in charge of water supply at KEMMEL village and is also carrying out improvements in the sanitary areas of this village. Four "P.B." men are detailed for these duties and are billetted in the village. **Water Supply.** Two drinking water stations viz. Nos 25 and 37 were kept open during the month and drinking water from unauthorised sources was available for all troops in this in the area. The New site about the middle of the month and repairs to the drinking water supply system were taken in hand by the 136 Co. R.E. Considerable damage having been done by the severe frost. The two water stations above were used extensively during the months by trains billetted on the right & left of this area, and half the drinking water issued was taken by units other than those belonging to this Division. Drinking Water Station No. 23 at KEMMEL SHELTERS was damaged by enemy artillery fire and this was reported at once to the IX Corps Water Board, but the appearance of the New SI was discovered that the felts in MONT KEMMEL were leaking and repairs were	

Army Form C. 2118.

Vol. XV
Sheet 2

WAR DIARY
or
INTELLIGENCE SUMMARY.
(Erase heading not required.)

Place	Date	Hour	Summary of Events and Information	Remarks and references to Appendices

taken in hand at once; at the same time the sand and gravel used in the filter were analysed. On Feb. 20th I submitted a report through A.D.M.S. 16th Division, on a possible auxiliary source of water supply at the BREWERY, KEMMEL VILLAGE for the consideration of IX Corps Water Board. The question of supply of 4 tins of Bleaching Powder for the sterilizing station of water service gone into with the Senior Supply Officer, 16th Division, a temporary shortage of the chemical having been reported; supplies are now normal again.

Constructional work good progress has been made during the month. A good deal of repair work to latrine incinerators has been done. New work has been done in KEMMEL VILLAGE & this village. New are no new form sanitary areas conveniently situated as regards the main billetting areas. Raised paths have been made to three of these latrine areas, and dry standings constructed in the latrines; it is proposed to construct concrete floors to the latrines during the coming month. A public urinal has been constructed in the centre of the village and an officers latrine in one of the sanitary areas. Other constructional work which has been completed during the month is enumerated below

(1) G. Hq. part latrine area made in the orchard traced to the 16th BAC

2353 Wt. W25441/1454 700,000 5/15 D. D. & L. A.D.S.S./Forms/C. 2118.

WAR DIARY
or
INTELLIGENCE SUMMARY.

Army Form C. 2118.

Vol XV
Sheet 3

Place	Date	Hour	Summary of Events and Information	Remarks and references to Appendices

(ii) Seven incinerators were made according to my design by the 16th Field R.E., were issued to Camp wardens in charge of infantry camps.

(iii) Refuse receptacles, made of wood & fine mesh expanded metal, were constructed in the workshop and issued.

(iv) An ablution shed was constructed in WESTOUTRE.

(v) 4 urine troughs were made in the workshop & issued.

(vi) An oven was built for use at the Officers Club LOCRE.

(vii) A small plant for filtering chlorinated water (for use in a small soya waters traction which is being installed by the Division at WESTOUTRE) was made by the Sections Sanitary Officer.

There was an increase in the number of cases of Infectious Diseases notified during the month. 13 cases of measles and 6 cases of German measles occurred in the Division in February as against 5 cases in January (2 measles, 3 German measles). In all cases disinfecting parties were despatched from Headquarters. I carried out enquiries into a number of cases of measles, & no cases of mumps in January. It was traced to drafts - who developed the disease a few days after arrival in the area - from No. 3 Infantry Camp ROUEN. It is possible that this was the starting point for the other cases.

Army Form C. 2118.

WAR DIARY
or
INTELLIGENCE SUMMARY.
(Erase heading not required.)

Place	Date	Hour	Summary of Events and Information	Remarks and references to Appendices
			Two cases of mumps occurred in February as against seven cases in January. A case of diphtheria occurred on Feb 1st, evidently contracted through the use by inmates of a farm and adjoining premises at which a fatal case of diphtheria had occurred (child, civilian). This farm adjoins the camp in which the case occurred. The farm was put out of bounds on Jan 29th. On the investigation of this case the usual are of No 5 Canadian Bacteriological Laboratory was obtained. A report on the case, and on the measures taken to prevent the spread of the disease, was submitted to ADMS 16th Division. On the 13th February three other cases occurred among the troops of the Division. Three other cases occurred among civilians during the month. In each case the house was placed out of bounds to all troops. Three cases of cerebrospinal meningitis occurred in the 1st Entrenching Battalion stationed at GARDEN FARM (28 SW. N. 13 d. 6. 1.) In each case the contacts were isolated and examined by O.C. No 5 Canadian Bacteriological Laboratory for the presence of the meningococcus in the naso-pharynx. All contacts were found to be negative. A careful investigation was made, but all efforts fails to reveal any likely common source of infection. The origin of the disease in these three cases thus remains undetermined; there is evidently a carrier or carriers in the unit. No cases occurred in other units in the Division or area.	

Army Form C. 2118.

WAR DIARY
or
INTELLIGENCE SUMMARY.
(Erase heading not required.)

Place	Date	Hour	Summary of Events and Information	Remarks and references to Appendices
			General. Lectures at the 16th Divisional School on Feb 1st, 2nd, 8th, 9th, 15th, 16th, 22nd and at the Ir. Corps School of Sanitation Feb 15th, 16th, 22nd & 23rd	

Percival Hurley
Capt. RAMC
O.C. 81st Sanitary Section

WAR DIARY
FOR MONTH OF MARCH, 1917.

VOLUME 16

UNIT:- 81st Sanitary Section R.A.M.C.

Army Form C. 2118.
Vol. XVI
Part 1

WAR DIARY
or
INTELLIGENCE SUMMARY.
(Erase heading not required.)

Place	Date	Hour	Summary of Events and Information	Remarks and references to Appendices
In the Field	March 1st to March 31st 1917		1. Location of Personnel of the Unit. The headquarters of the 17th Sanitary Section remained at WESTOUTRE during the month; a detachment was maintained as usual at LOCRE for work in the eastern section of the Divisional area. On March 13th, a party of 4 men, one drawn from headquarters and three from the LOCRE detachment, were pushed to the BERTHEN training area for duty with the 47th Infantry Brigade. On March 22nd, in accordance with instructions from A.D.M.S. 16th Division, 2 men were detailed for duty in connection with units from the 19th Division. The sergeant of the section has been lent to D.D.M.S. IX Corps for sanitary duties in connection with the new IX Corps Headquarters at MONT NOIR. One corporal of the unit was evacuated sick on March 28th 1917. 2. Water Supplies. During the month repairs to drinking water stations Nº 23 and 24 were completed and these stations are now in working order again. Repairs to drinking water station Nº 36 are also complete and the station is ready for use when required. Repairs to drinking water station Nº 21 and the MONT KEMMEL Supply are almost complete and these supplies are expected to be available for use again in a few days time. Repairs to installations and representations to the IX Corps	

A.D.S.S./Forms/C. 2118.

WAR DIARY or INTELLIGENCE SUMMARY

Army Form C. 2118

Place	Date	Hour	Summary of Events and Information	Remarks and references to Appendices

concerning the use of drinking Water Station No 25 by heavy motor lorries has been unavailing.

3. Construction work has been progress has been made; the following work has been done during the week.

Fly proof latrines have been constructed for the use of the following units troops
LOCRE (public latrine, 10 seats) 47th Indian Lines Coys (4 seats) 112th Field Ambulance Advanced Dressing Station (4 seats) 3 for the 6th Gurkhas latrine Battalion (2 will 2 seats + 1 with one seat) officers club LOCRE (1 seat) Headquarters 177 Brigade R.F.A. (1 seat) D/177 Brigade R.F.A. (1 seat) Officers latrine KEMMEL VILLAGE (2 seats) 19th Motor Machine Gun Coys (1 seat). Iron Company brewer fly proof latrines were supplied to the 19th D.S.C. and one brass fly proof latrine is in course of construction for use of Headquarters troops at NETTOUTRE. Repairs here carried out to 5 latrines at KEMMEL which had been damaged by shell fire and the erection of the floors to the latrines at KEMMEL is in progress.

Mine troops tunnels were constructed for the use of the following units or Camps:- KEMMEL VILLAGE, DONCASTER HUTS, 7th Royal Irish Rifles, Brasserie

WAR DIARY
INTELLIGENCE SUMMARY.

(Transport lines) 16th Sivil Arm. Stan., 16th S.A.C., BERTHEN training area. 16th DHQ, 6th Sudan Labour Batt., 19th S.J.C. BIRR BARRACKS.

One brick incinerator for burning faeces was constructed in KEMMEL VILLAGE and one brick incinerator for the same purpose is in course of construction at LOCRE. Grease traps were constructed and installed at BIRR BARRACKS and in the Camp of the 6th Sudan Labour Battalion. One field urine tin was built for the use of the Officers Club LOCRE. Twelve night urine pails were made + issued for use of BIRR BARRACKS. One reed safe made + issued for use of a headquarters here, 16th Division.

4. Infectious disease. There has been an increase in the number of cases of infectious disease during the week. Twenty cases of measles, 25 of German measles, 7 of mumps and one of cerebrospinal meningitis were notified as against 13 cases of measles, 6 of German measles, 2 of mumps and 3 of cerebrospinal meningitis notified in February. One case of scarlet fever and one of Para typhoid B were also notified during the month. Transfer of billets to town carried out when necessary.

Army Form C. 2118.

WAR DIARY
INTELLIGENCE SUMMARY.
(Erase heading not required.)

Vol. XVI
theet 4

Place	Date	Hour	Summary of Events and Information	Remarks and references to Appendices
(S)General.			I lectured at the 16th Division School on March 12th and at the IX Corps School of Sanitation on March 1st, 2nd, 8th, 19th, 1917	

Percival Hartley
Capt. R.A.M.C.T.
ADMS 61st Sanitary Section

www.ingramcontent.com/pod-product-compliance
Lightning Source LLC
Chambersburg PA
CBHW081443160426
43193CB00013B/2373